CAITLIN CLARK

THIS EDITION

Produced for DK by WonderLab Group LLC
Jennifer Emmett, Erica Green, Kate Hale, *Founders*

Editor Maya Myers; **Photography Editor** Nicole DiMella; **Managing Editor** Rachel Houghton;
Designers Project Design Company; **Researcher** Michelle Harris; **Copy Editor** Lori Merritt;
Indexer Connie Binder; **Proofreader** Susan K. Hom; **Series Reading Specialist** Dr. Jennifer Albro

First American Edition, 2025
Published in the United States by DK Publishing, a division of Penguin Random House LLC
1745 Broadway, 20th Floor, New York, NY 10019

Published in Great Britain by Dorling Kindersley Limited

HC ISBN 978-0-5939-6815-4
PB ISBN 978-0-5939-6814-7

DK books are available at special discounts when purchased in bulk for sales promotions, premiums, fund-raising, or educational use.
For details, contact:
DK Publishing Special Markets, 1745 Broadway, 20th Floor, New York, NY 10019
SpecialSales@dk.com

Printed and bound in Canada

Super Readers Lexile® levels 620L to 790L Lexile® is the registered trademark of MetaMetrics, Inc.
Copyright © 2024 MetaMetrics, Inc. All rights reserved.

The publisher would like to thank the following for their kind permission to reproduce their images:
a=above; c=center; b=below; l=left; r=right; t=top; b/g=background
Alamy Stock Photo: Cal Sport Media / Jeff Halstead 33cr, 35crb, Patti McConville 44tr, Sipa US / Efren Landaos 43, ZUMA Press Wire / Scott Rausenberger 15, ZUMA Press, Inc. 44tc, ZUMA Press, Inc. / Steven Garcia 22; **Derek Brooks:** 29bc; **Dreamstime.com:** Fotokitas 18b, Joseph Helfenberger 18t, Monkey Business Images 20cr, Skypixel 13br, Daniel Thornberg 7, Elena Titova 24b; **Getty Images:** Steph Chambers 4-5, Steph Chambers 33cl, 35cl, Steph Chambers 36, G Fiume 33clb, 35bl, Luke Hales 45, Michael Hickey 38, Michael Hickey 41, Matthew Holst 12t, Matthew Holst 19, Matthew Holst 28-29c, Matthew Holst 30, Matthew Holst 32, Matthew Holst 35, Matthew Holst 37br, Icon Sportswire 33crb, Ron Jenkins 8, Mitchell Layton 35clb, Andy Lyons 32bl, Andy Lyons 39br, Andy Lyons 40, Maddie Meyer 6, Maddie Meyer 9, Maddie Meyer 25, Ethan Miller 3, 10, Jason Miller 37cr, NCAA Photos / C. Morgan Engel 1, NCAA Photos / Rich Clarkson 35cr, Michael Reaves 16tr, Michael Reaves 31cl, Joe Robbins 26cr, Gregory Shamus 14cr, Sportico 39tr, Sarah Stier 11, Sarah Stier 31t, The Washington Post 16b, Aaron J. Thornton 28cl; **IMAGN:** © Bryon Houlgrave - USA TODAY NETWORK 16tl, © Bryon Houlgrave - USA TODAY NETWORK 20tl, © Dylan Heuer - USA TODAY NETWORK 21, © Joseph Cress - USA TODAY NETWORK 12-13, © Joseph Cress / Iowa City Press-Citizen via Imagn Content Services, LLC 27, © Rodney White - USA TODAY NETWORK 14cl, © The Indianapolis Star-USA TODAY NETWORK 42, © Zach Boyden-Holmes - USA TODAY NETWORK 23; **Shutterstock.com:** Eduardo Medrano 24c

Cover images: *Front:* **Dreamstime.com:** Sgursozlu cl; **Getty Images:** G Fiume; *Back:* **Dreamstime.com:** Pikepicture cl; **Shutterstock.com:** luma_art cra

www.dk.com

MIX
Paper | Supporting
responsible forestry
FSC™ C018179

This book was made with Forest Stewardship Council™ certified paper – one small step in DK's commitment to a sustainable future.
Learn more at www.dk.com/uk/information/sustainability

CAITLIN CLARK

Ellen Labrecque

Contents

6   Simply the Best

14   An Athletic Childhood

20   The Recruit

26   Home Is Where the Hoop Is

38   Welcome to the WNBA

42   The Caitlin Clark Effect

46 Glossary

47 Index

48 Quiz

Simply the Best

On March 31, 2023, junior point guard Caitlin Clark stepped onto the wood floor at the American Airlines Center in Dallas, Texas. The game was sold out. More than 19,000 fans were ready to watch Clark's team, the University of Iowa Hawkeyes. The Hawkeyes were facing the South Carolina Gamecocks.

Clark driving past South Carolina's Brea Beal

March Madness

March Madness is a single elimination tournament for both men's and women's college basketball teams. Sixty-eight teams compete in the tournament. At first, four teams are eliminated. As the tournament goes on, more teams are eliminated. The final rounds are called the Sweet Sixteen, the Elite Eight, the Final Four, and the National Championship game.

This was a big game in the Final Four of the March Madness college basketball tournament. Fans believed South Carolina would easily beat Iowa. The Gamecocks were the defending national champions. They had won their last 42 games in a row!

But Clark and her teammates had other plans. The Hawkeyes won the game, 77–73!

The final buzzer went off. Clark tossed the ball into the air. Then, she put a hand to her ear. Iowa fans responded with a collective roar. One fan held up a sign that read, "In Clark we trust." Clark finished the game with 41 points, eight assists, and six rebounds. She made five three-pointers.

"I think she's the most phenomenal basketball player in America," said Iowa head coach Lisa Bluder.

Coach Bluder was right. Clark is a phenomenal basketball player—maybe the best ever. Clark played for four years at the University of Iowa (2020–2024). She finished her college career with 3,951 points. That's more points than any other college basketball player ever!

On April 15, 2024, the Indiana Fever selected Clark as the number-one pick in the WNBA Draft. Over three million fans watched on TV—the most viewers in draft history.

Clark was picked number one for many reasons. She is a scoring machine. She can score from anywhere on the court. She is especially good at making shots far away from the hoop. Clark can also drive to the basket. She makes layups with two or even three defenders trying to stop her. When Clark isn't making shots, she is tossing no-look or behind-the-back passes to her teammates.

Chelsea Gray in the 2023 WNBA All-Star Game

The WNBA
The WNBA (Women's National Basketball Association) has twelve teams, including the Indiana Fever. The teams are split into two conferences of six. The regular season runs from May until September.

WNBA Commissioner Cathy Engelbert presenting Clark with a Fever jersey during the 2024 WNBA Draft

Clark is a clutch player. She is at her best when the score is close. The more pressure there is, the better Clark plays.

Clark is a special player. Everybody wants to watch her play. On October 15, 2023, Clark's Iowa team played DePaul University at the Kinnick Stadium in Iowa City. There were 55,646 fans in the football stadium.

Clark shooting over DePaul's Charlece Ohiaeri

This was the most ever at a women's college basketball game! Clark was the main attraction.

How did she become one of the best and most popular players of all time?

An Athletic Childhood

When she was five years old, Clark played a pretend game with her mom. Clark hid in the closet. Her mom acted like a basketball announcer. "Now starting for the Iowa Hawkeyes, Caitie Clark," her mom said in a booming voice. Her mom opened the closet door, and young Caitie ran out ready to play. Even then, Clark knew she wanted to become a basketball star.

Clark and her mother, Anne

Clark at home with her brother Colin

Clark and her brothers, Blake (left) and Colin (right) after the 2024 NCAA Tournament

Caitlin Clark was born on January 22, 2002. Her family lives in Des Moines [duh MOYN], Iowa. She is the middle child in her family. She has an older brother named Blake. Her younger brother is named Colin. Clark and her brothers played many different sports, including football, softball, and soccer. And of course, basketball.

Clark was competitive in everything she did—at school, at home, and in the gym. Clark did not just play basketball. She played a lot of sports. She played against girls and boys. Clark knew doing different activities made her a better athlete. The variety made her physically and mentally stronger. It made her a better basketball player in the long run.

"I think it was super special in my development," Clark said. "It was just like, I'm a girl, I can hold my own. This is not anything I've been afraid of."

Clark began to play on organized sports teams when she was five years old. She played on a boys' basketball team. Clark was so good, an opponent's parent complained. They said a girl should not be allowed to play with boys!

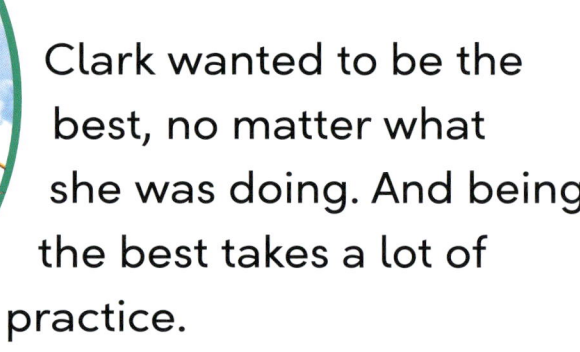

Clark wanted to be the best, no matter what she was doing. And being the best takes a lot of practice.

Clark shot hoops in her driveway. She practiced shooting farther and farther from the basket. Her dad got rid of some grass to make the driveway bigger.

When Clark was in sixth grade, she joined an AAU (Amateur Athletic Union) girls' basketball team. College coaches started to recruit Clark. Each of them hoped she would go to their college and play on their team.

Long Range

At the top of the arch, the college three-point line is 22 feet 1.75 inches (6.75 m) away from the basket. Clark shoots from four or even five feet behind the line!

Clark and her family

Clark's mom and dad thought it was too early for her to think about college. They didn't tell her about the letters she received from coaches almost every day.

"My parents were like, this is not the kind of stuff a seventh grader should be thinking about," explained Clark.

After all, she hadn't even played in high school yet!

The Recruit

In the fall of 2016, Clark began her first year at Dowling Catholic High School in West Des Moines. She started on the varsity team as a first-year. During her junior and senior years, Clark led the state of Iowa in scoring. She averaged 32.6 points per game as a junior and 33.4 points as a senior.

Making the Grade

In high school, students have names that go with the grade they're in:

Ninth graders are called first-years or freshmen.
Tenth graders are called sophomores.
Eleventh graders are called juniors.
Twelfth graders are called seniors.

In college, students are also called first-years/freshmen, sophomores, juniors, and seniors.

Clark playing for Dowling Catholic in 2019

During one game, Clark dropped 60 points in a 90–78 victory over Mason City High School. It was the second-highest single-game point total in Iowa girls' basketball history.

Clark passing behind her back away from Michigan's Elissa Brett

Clark didn't only shoot for the basket. She was also a talented passer. At first, her high school coach, Kristin Meyer, thought her passes were too fancy.

In one game, Clark threw a behind-the-back pass. It worked, but her coach had a rule. If Clark threw a behind-the-back pass and one of her teammates caught it, she could throw another one. But if she threw one that resulted in a turnover, she would not be allowed to do another one. Clark never turned the ball over on any behind-the-back passes, not once!

Clark plays better when her family is in the stands. In one high school game, she was not playing her best. Her brother Blake arrived late. As soon as Blake got there, Clark's game suddenly got better. She scored 30 points in the second half. Her brother cheered her on.

"I don't think people really understand how important her home, her family, her community really is to her," said Clark's mom.

Clark's family cheering her on

College coaches from around the country aggressively recruited Clark. They tried to convince her to come play on their teams. By her sophomore year, Clark was one of the top women's basketball recruits in the country.

University of Iowa

IOWA

Des Moines

Iowa City

At first, Clark thought she would attend the University of Notre Dame. Notre Dame is near South Bend, Indiana. That's about a six-hour drive from Clark's hometown of Des Moines. Clark visited Notre Dame. But she felt too far away from her family and friends. Clark decided to attend the University of Iowa in Iowa City. It was less than two hours from her hometown.

"I wanted to stay close and do something special," Clark explained.

Home Is Where the Hoop Is

In 2020, Clark's college career tipped off with an awesome first-year. She led the NCAA Division I in scoring with 26.6 points per game. Iowa made it to the Sweet Sixteen in the NCAA tournament.

That year, Clark was also third in the nation in assists. She had seven assists per game. An assist is when a player passes the ball to another player who then scores.

Top NCAA Teams
The National Collegiate Athletic Association (NCAA) is an organization of college sports throughout the US. As of 2024, here are the top five programs that have won the most NCAA Division I women's basketball titles:
University of Connecticut (11)
University of Tennessee (8)
Baylor University (3)
Stanford University (3)
University of South Carolina (3)

UConn celebrating their 2016 national title

Clark dishes no-look and behind-the-back passes in almost every game. She makes passes that other players don't even see are there.

At first, Clark got frustrated with teammates if they missed one of her sneaky passes. Iowa Coach Lisa Bluder talked to Clark. She told her she needed to support her teammates instead of getting mad at them. This was a wake-up call for Clark. She did not just want to be a great player. She also wanted to be a great teammate.

Iowa playing Rutgers in 2020

As a sophomore, Clark again led the NCAA in scoring. She had 27 points per game. She also led in assists, with eight per game. She began making longer and longer shots.

Clark shooting over Michigan's Laila Phelia in 2022

In one game, Iowa trailed the University of Michigan by as much as 25 points. Then, Clark began hitting every shot. In the final six minutes, Clark hit four three-pointers and scored 21 points. Michigan won, but Clark scored 46 points. Her performance rocketed her into stardom.

Clark had another remarkable season as a junior. The Final Four game against the University of South Carolina was Clark's biggest game yet. South Carolina was expected to win, but Iowa beat them, 77–73. Clark shined.

"Once you make a few shots, the basket looks super big," Clark said with a smile.

Clark became more and more famous. Companies wanted her to appear in ads for their products. They paid her a lot of money.

A life-size Caitlin Clark butter sculpture at the Iowa State Fair, 2023

Clark began her senior year in the fall of 2023. She had already scored 2,717 points in college. She needed 811 more points to break the NCAA Division I women's basketball scoring record. And if she got 951 points, she'd become the all-time leading scorer for both men and women.

Fans believed Clark could break both these records. Everybody wanted to be there to see this. Every home game was sold out. So were most of their away games.

Clark signing autographs in 2024

The stands were filled with young girls and boys wearing Clark's jersey. Clark spent time after every game signing autographs. She high-fived young fans. Clark was thrilled with the attention. It wasn't just good for her. It was important to her teammates and all of women's college basketball.

"When Caitlin's light shines, it shines on all of us," Coach Bluder said.

The celebration after Clark broke the NCAA women's all-time scoring record

On February 15, 2024, Iowa faced the University of Michigan at home. The sold-out game was the hottest ticket in the country. Clark needed just eight points to become the women's all-time top scorer. Everybody wanted to see her make history.

Clark did not disappoint. She was on fire from the tip-off. She scored her first two points on a layup. Then she swished a three-pointer. One more three-pointer and she'd set the record.

Clark ran up the court and shot from 33 feet away. Score! Clark was now the women's all-time leading scorer! Clark finished with 49 points, 13 assists, and five rebounds. She set the University of Iowa record for most points in a single game. Clark was the biggest story in all of sports.

Women's Division I NCAA Top Career Scorers

Player	School	Point Total	Year
Caitlin Clark	University of Iowa	3,951	2024
Kelsey Plum	University of Washington	3,527	2017
Dyaisha Fair	Syracuse University	3,403	2024
Kelsey Mitchell	Ohio State University	3,402	2018
Jackie Stiles	Missouri State University	3,393	2001

March 3, 2024, was Iowa's final game of the regular season. The game was sold out once again. People all over the world were watching on TV.

Clark needed 18 points to break the NCAA Division I all-time scoring record. Pete Maravich of Louisiana State University had held the record for 54 years.

Iowa was ranked sixth in the nation. Their opponent, Ohio State, was ranked second. It was almost halftime. Clark made a foul shot. It was her 3,668th college point. She had broken Maravich's record.

The crowd went wild. And Clark kept scoring through the second half. She had 35 points, made nine assists, and grabbed six rebounds. Iowa beat Ohio State, 93–83.

"None of this would have been possible without my family and friends who have been by my side through it all," Clark said after the game.

NCAA Division 1 Top Career Scorers

Player	School	Point Total	Year
Caitlin Clark	University of Iowa	3,951	2024
Pete Maravich	Louisiana State University	3,667	1970
Antoine Davis	University of Detroit Mercy	3,664	2023
Kelsey Plum	University of Washington	3,527	2017
Dyaisha Fair	Buffalo/Syracuse	3,403	2024

During the 2024 NCAA national championship game

On April 7, 2024, Iowa played in the national championship game again. They faced South Carolina like they had in the Final Four the year before. More than 24 million people watched the game on TV. It was the most-watched women's college basketball game ever. Clark had 30 points and eight rebounds. But South Carolina came out on top this time, 87–75.

Clark had played in her last college game. She was the NCAA Division I all-time leading scorer. She also finished her college career with many other women's records.

She scored the most points in a single NCAA season: 1,234. She made the most career three-pointers in NCAA tournament history: 78. She also had the most career assists in NCAA tournament history: 152. Clark's impact on the game was already massive, and her professional career hadn't even begun.

Dawn Staley was the South Carolina head coach. "I want to personally thank Caitlin Clark for lifting up our sport," Staley said after the championship game. "So, Caitlin Clark, if you're out there, you are one of the GOATs of our game, and we appreciate you."

Dawn Staley

GOAT

GOAT is a sports slang term. When a player is called a GOAT, it means they are considered the Greatest of All Time. Michael Jordan and LeBron James are two of the GOATs of the NBA (National Basketball Association). Gymnast Simone Biles and tennis player Serena Williams are GOATs in their sports, too.

Welcome to the WNBA

The 2024 WNBA draft was held on April 15. Everyone expected Clark to be selected first, and she was.

The Indiana Fever selected Clark as the number-one pick. Clark hugged her mom and dad and brothers. The next chapter of Clark's career was about to begin.

Clark's Indiana Fever jersey sold out within hours. The WNBA also announced that thirty-six of the Fever's forty games would be televised nationally. That's more than any other WNBA team's games. No matter where Clark plays, fans want to watch.

Clark driving past Seattle's Victoria Vivans

During Clark's first season, she became the first rookie in WNBA history to record a triple-double (19 points, 13 assists, 12 rebounds). She also broke the WNBA single-game assist record (19) and tied the rookie record for most three-pointers in a game (seven). More fans attended every single game for the Fever than they had in any other season.

Clark had to adjust to the physical play of the WNBA. Opponents pushed and pulled at her much harder than they had in college. And because Clark was so popular, it sometimes seemed like she was treated worse than other players. At times, opponents fouled her harder than they should. Clark just played through it. She said she would "let her play do the talking."

Clark being guarded by New York's Breanna Stewart

The Caitlin Clark Effect

Caitlin Clark's fame continues to grow. Her image was on a giant billboard in the middle of Times Square in New York City. Caitlin Clark murals and banners have been painted in Iowa City and in Indianapolis, home of the Fever. She appears on talk shows. She stars in national commercials.

Artist Kwazar Martin finishing a mural of Clark in March 2024

Clark and fellow newly drafted WNBA players atop the Empire State Building, 2024

On April 13, 2024, Clark appeared on the famous comedy show *Saturday Night Live*. On the show, Clark was playful. She told a lot of jokes, but she also said something serious.

Clark thanked several great players who had come before her. She said that these women had "kicked down the door so I could walk inside."

She is thankful for all the great women athletes who came before her.

The impact Caitlin Clark has made on the game will last forever. Clark has increased excitement and enthusiasm for women's basketball. She broke record after record at the college level. She may do the same thing at the professional level. Clark makes longer three-pointers than any other WNBA player before her has.

When Iowa retired Clark's number 22 jersey, they said that there will never be another Caitlin Clark. This is definitely the case. But Clark knows other great players will follow her.

"I want my legacy to be the impact I can have on young kids," Clark said. "When I think about women's basketball going forward, obviously it's just going to continue to grow... Everybody sees it. Everybody knows."

Caitlin Clark will always be a big reason why this is so.

Glossary

Aggressively
In a determined and forceful way

Clutch
Extremely good under extreme pressure

Collective
Done by people acting as a group

Competitive
Eager to do better than others; always wanting to win

Dish
To pass the ball

Draft
The process through which a team selects or choses players to join their team

Frustrated
Feeling distressed or annoyed

Impact
To have a strong effect

Layup
A one-handed shot made from near the basket

Mural
A painting or other work of art on a wall

Opponent
A person on the other team

Organized
Structured and following a defined set of rules

Phenomenal
Remarkable, extraordinary

Recruit
To encourage a player to join a team or program

Rookie
A player in their first season with a team

Talented
Having a special ability to do something well

Tip-off
The beginning of play in a basketball game

Turnover
When a player from one team unintentionally gives possession of the ball to the opposing team

Index

AAU (Amateur Athletic Union) 18

assists 8, 26, 28, 33, 34, 37, 40

Beal, Brea 6

Biles, Simone 37

Bluder, Lisa 9, 27, 31

Brett, Elissa 22

Clark, Caitlin
  behind-the-back passes 10, 22, 27
  childhood 14–19
  college career 6–9, 26, 28, 30–37
  college recruitment 18–19, 24–25
  fame 29, 42–43
  family 14, 15, 18, 19, 23, 38
  fans 12, 30–31, 39, 40
  high school 20–24
  legacy 44–45
  practice 18
  teamwork 10, 22, 27
  WNBA career 10, 11, 38–42

Davis, Antoine 35

Dowling Catholic High School 20–24

draft 10, 11, 38, 39

Engelbert, Cathy 11

Fair, Dyaisha 33, 35

GOAT 37

Gray, Chelsea 10

Indiana Fever 10, 38–42

James, LeBron 37

Jordan, Michael 37

Maravich, Pete 34, 35

March Madness 6–8, 15, 26, 29, 36

Martin, Kwazar 42

Meyer, Kristin 22

Mitchell, Kelsey 33

NBA (National Basketball Association) 37

NCAA
  Clark's statistics 8, 9, 20, 26, 28, 30–37
  March Madness tournament 6–8, 15, 26, 29, 36
  top teams 26

Ohiaeri, Charlece 13

Phelia, Laila 28

Plum, Kelsey 33, 35

Saturday Night Live 43

South Carolina Gamecocks 6–8, 26, 29, 36, 37

Staley, Dawn 37

Stewart, Breanna 41

Stiles, Jackie 33

three-point shots 8, 18, 28, 32, 37, 40, 44

University of Iowa Hawkeyes 6–9, 12–13, 24–36, 44

Vivans, Victoria 40

Williams, Serena 37

WNBA (Women's National Basketball Association) 10, 11, 38–42

Quiz

Answer the questions to see what you have learned. Check your answers in the key below.

1. What shot is Caitlin Clark most famous for shooting?

2. Where did Clark grow up?

3. Clark chose to attend the University of Iowa. What was the main reason for her choice?

4. Clark has been called the GOAT. What does this term mean?

5. True or False: Another Iowa player can wear Clark's number, 22, in the future.

1. A really long three-point shot 2. Des Moines, Iowa 3. She wanted to stay close to home. 4. Greatest of All Time 5. False